SOUTHWEST
INDIAN DESIGNS
Coloring Book

DIANNE GASPAS

DOVER PUBLICATIONS, INC.
Mineola, New York

NOTE

With a history reaching back 11,000 years, the American Indians of the southwestern United States have developed distinctive artistic styles to reflect and complement their rich culture. Drawing from the resources found in their environment, the Southwest Indians created clothing, tools, art, and goods from natural materials, using decorative patterns and motifs—many of which are unique to each tribe—to celebrate their spiritual beliefs and strong connection to nature. Kachina dolls, for example, are ornamented representations of spirits that inhabit various aspects of life, such as crops, animals, and stars. Through changing times and difficult circumstances, the Southwest Indians have managed to preserve their heritage by continuing their time-honored practices and passing their knowledge and artistry down to new generations.

The thirty plates in this book feature elaborate designs inspired by Southwest Indian art and artifacts. When available, names of the tribes that created the original work have been included, as well as the region where it was found.

Copyright

Copyright © 2003 by Dover Publications, Inc.
All rights reserved.

Bibliographical Note

Southwest Indian Designs Coloring Book is a new work, first published by
Dover Publications, Inc., in 2003.

International Standard Book Number

ISBN-13: 978-0-486-43042-3
ISBN-10: 0-486-43042-1

Manufactured in the United States by RR Donnelley
43042107   2015
www.doverpublications.com

Laguna Pueblo: Motif from jar (northwestern New Mexico)

PLATE 1

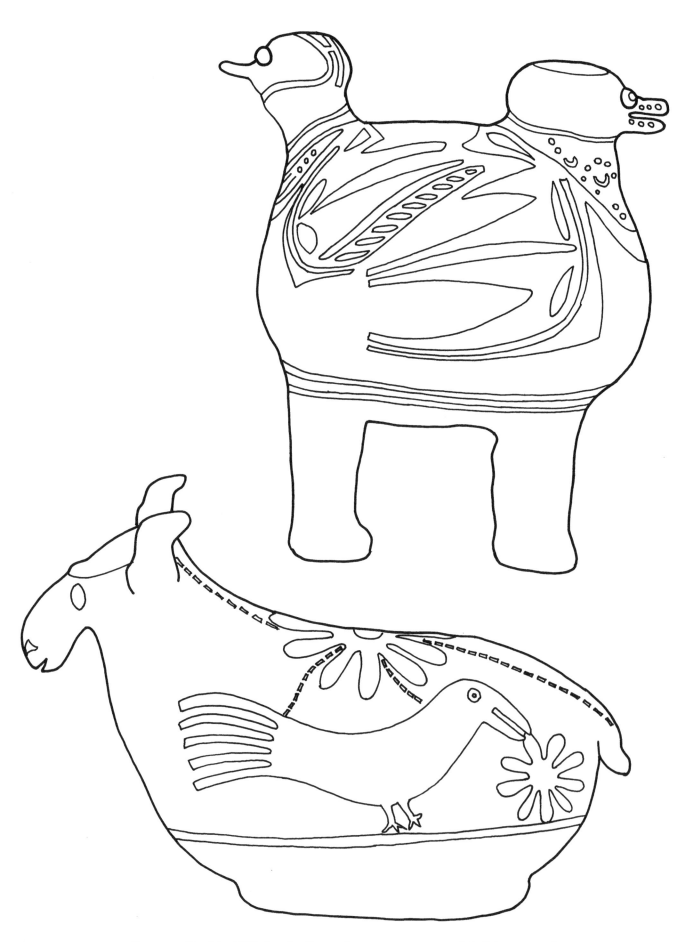

Laguna Pueblo: Effigies hollowed out to serve as drinking vessels
(western pueblo in northwestern New Mexico)

PLATE 2

Santo Domingo: Motif from jar (Rio Grande region, northwestern New Mexico)

PLATE 3

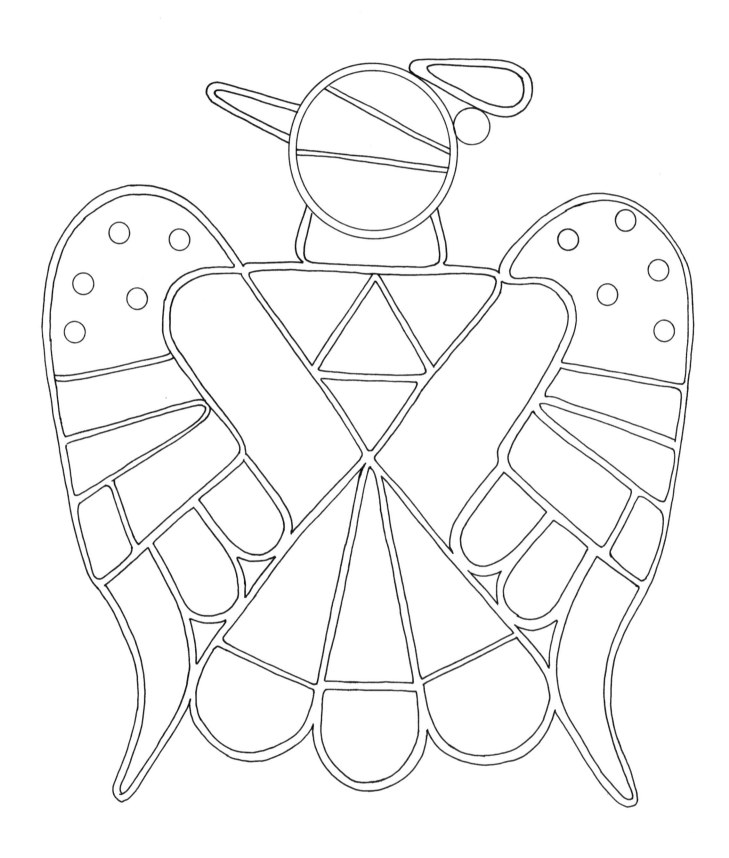

Modern *Zuni:* Mosaic of white shell, red oyster, black cannel coal, and turquoise

PLATE 4

Zuni Pueblo: Mask of Hemishikwe, worn for autumn festivals

PLATE 5

Zuni Pueblo: Shield

PLATE 6

Mimbres: Circular design (New Mexico and Arizona, 9th to 12th centuries)

PLATE 7

Mimbres: Design from pottery

PLATE 8

Mimbres: Design painted on inside of pottery bowl (New Mexico and Arizona, 9th to 12th centuries)

PLATE 9

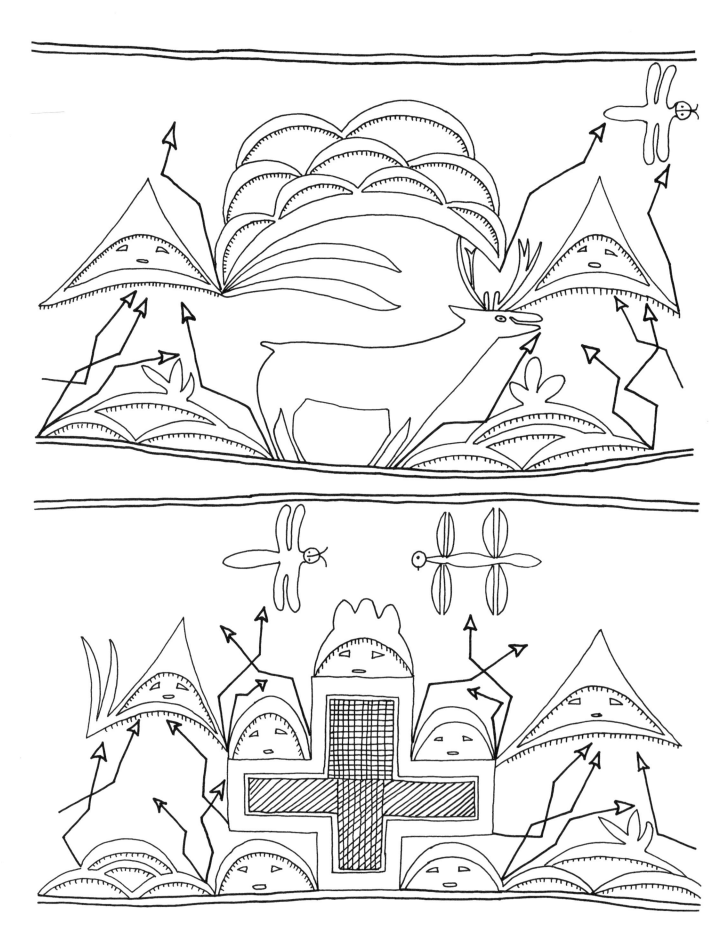

Sia Pueblo: Design from ceremonial water vase (upper and lower bands are one continuous design)

PLATE 10

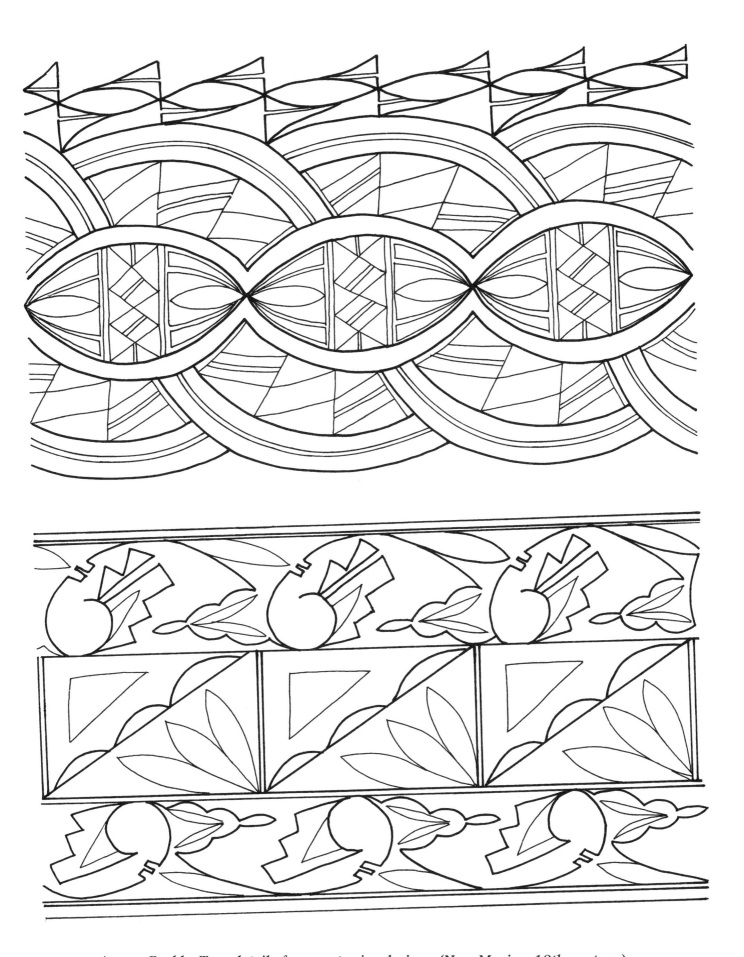

Acoma Pueblo: Two details from water jar designs (New Mexico, 19th century)

PLATE 11

Acoma Pueblo: Motif from jar (northwest New Mexico)

PLATE 12

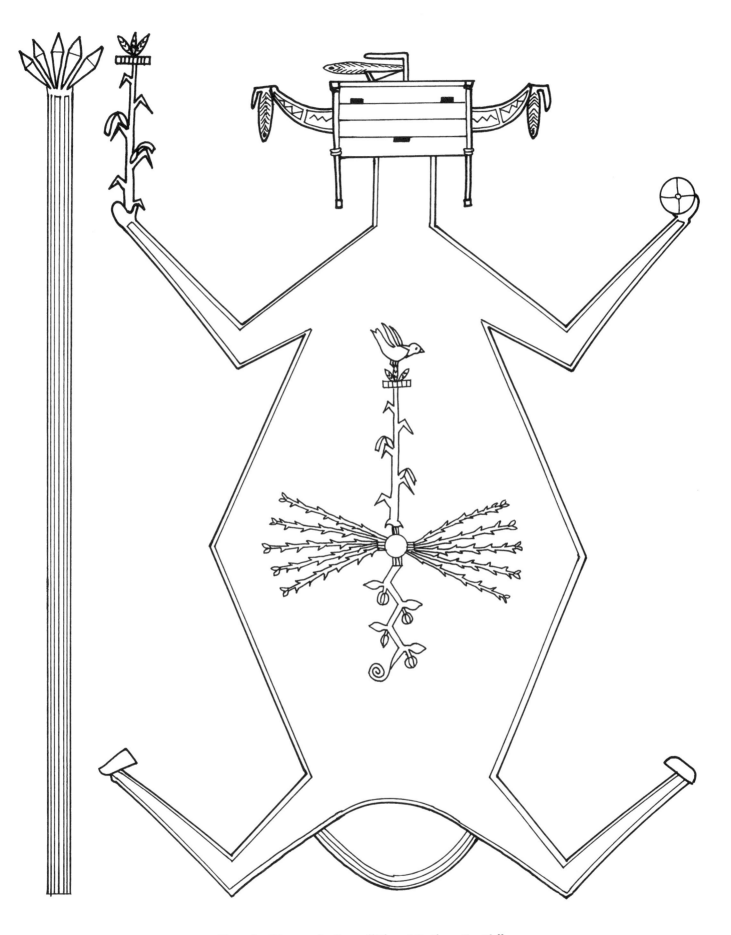

Navajo: Dry painting, "Blue Mother Earth"

PLATE 13

Navajo: Design from chief's blanket

PLATE 14

Navajo: Design from woven saddlebag

PLATE 15

Chumash: Rock painting (San Emigdiano Range)

PLATE 16

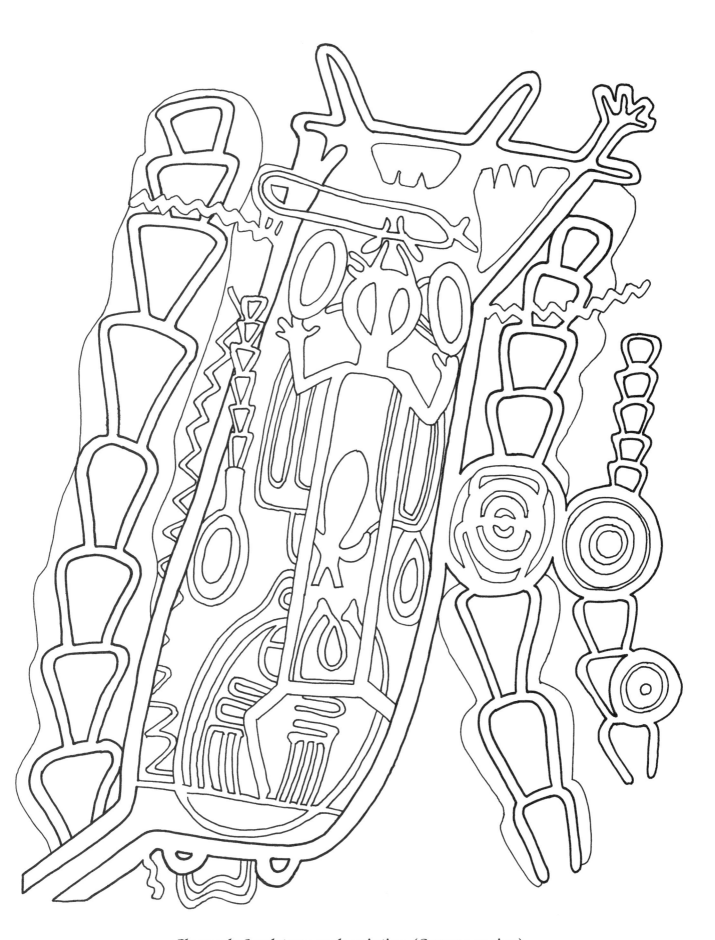

Chumash: Sandstone rock painting (Cuyama region)

PLATE 17

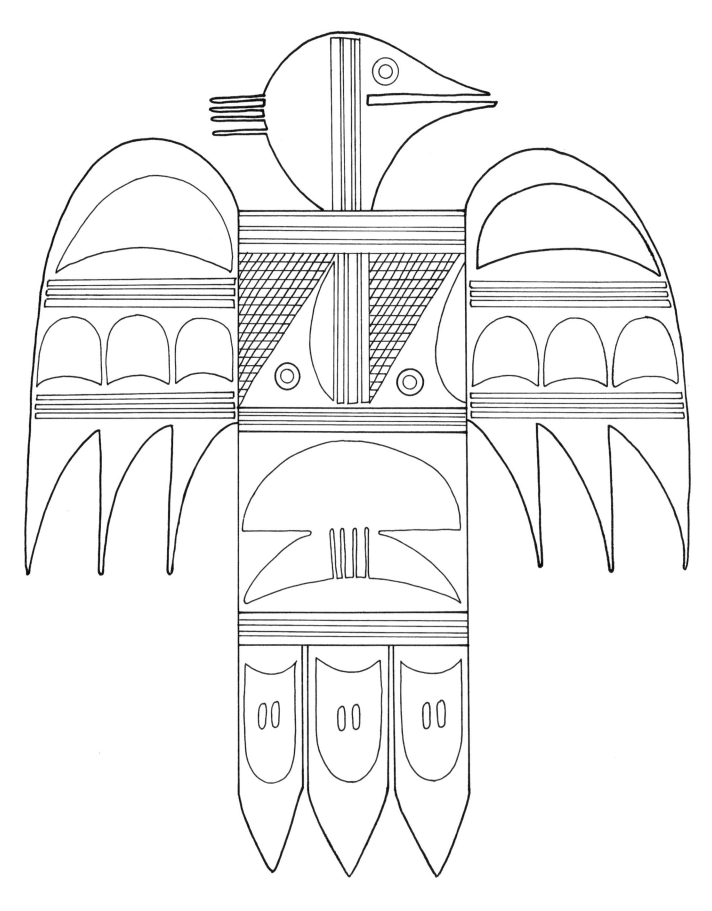

Hopi: Design from inside of bowl (Arizona)

PLATE 18

Hopi: Kachina doll representing Avatshoya, a god who facilitates germination of corn seed

PLATE 19

Hopi: Kachina doll representing Ahöla, a chief who brings prayers for a healthy life

PLATE 20

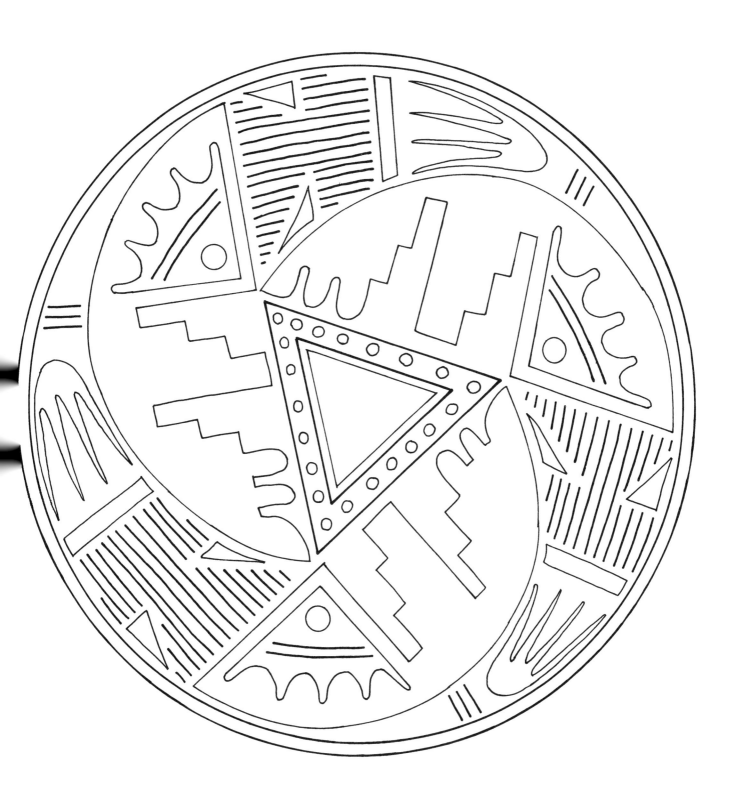

San Ildefonso Pueblo: Design from pottery bowl (Rio Grande region, New Mexico)

PLATE 21

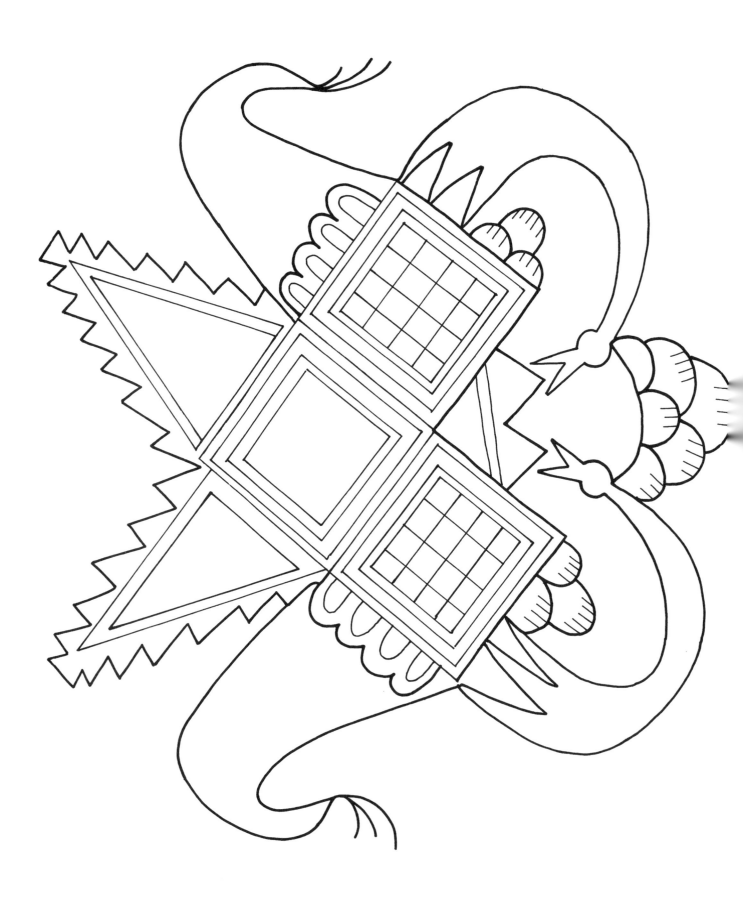

San Ildefonso Pueblo: Design from pottery

PLATE 22

Sikyatki: Animal design combining bird and reptile, possibly from the interior of a bowl (Arizona)

PLATE 23

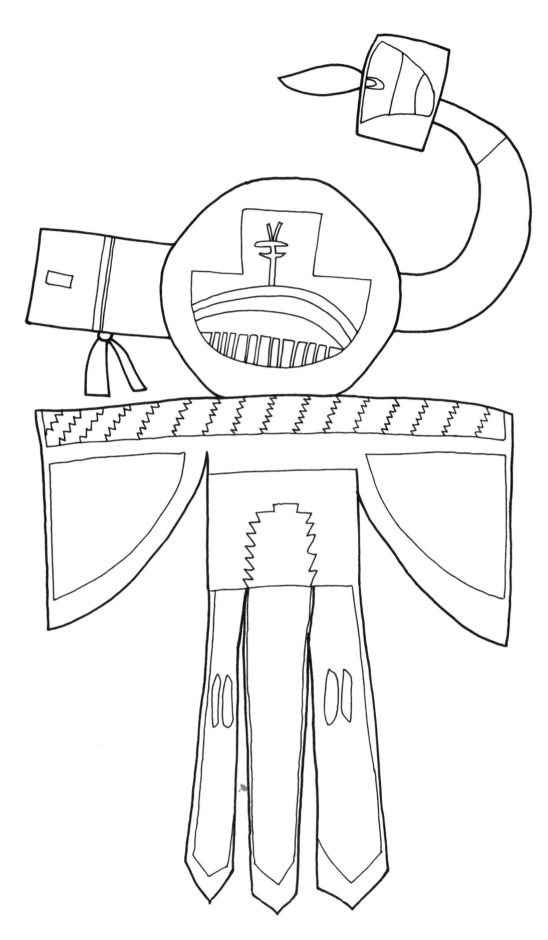

Hopi: Bird design from bowl found in ruins of old Shumopovi

PLATE 24

Pueblo: Bird design on pottery

PLATE 25

Cochiti: Hunting scene on pottery

PLATE 26

Apache: Rawhide playing card design

PLATE 27

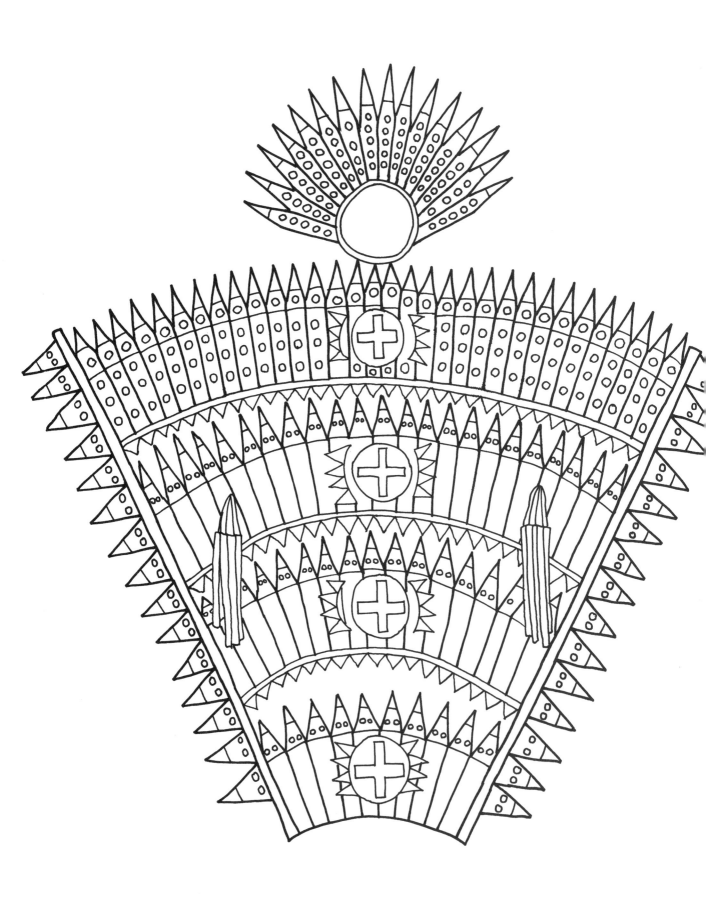

Apache: Crown headdress with crosses to indicate the four prime directions

PLATE 28

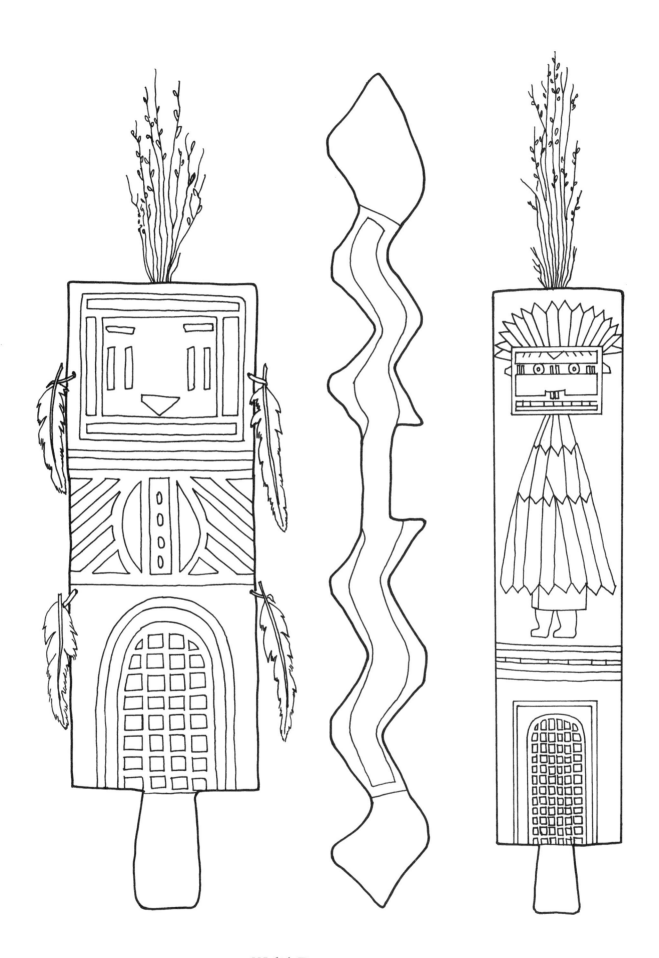

Walpi: Dance ornaments

PLATE 29

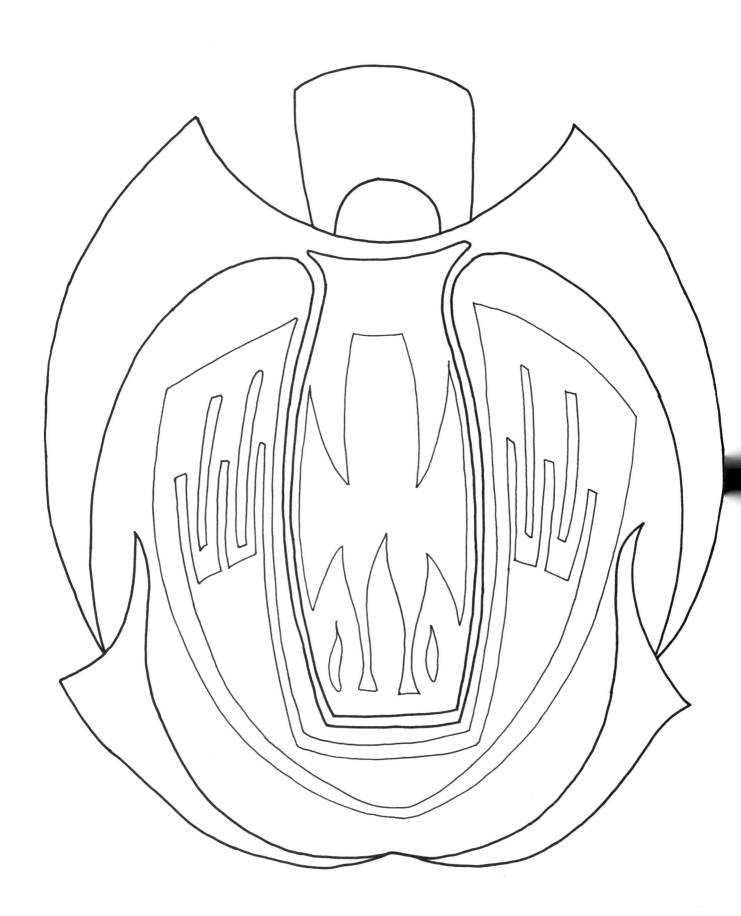

Sikyatki: Design from pottery (northeastern Arizona)

PLATE 30